PARES SCALES

For Individual Study
and Like-Instrument Class Instruction

by GABRIEL PARÈS

Revised and Edited by Harvey S. Whistler

Published for:

Flute or Piccolo . . . . Parès-Whistler

Clarinet . . . . Parès-Whistler

Oboe . . . . Parès-Whistler

Bassoon . . . . Parès-Whistler

Saxophone . . . . Parès-Whistler

Cornet, Trumpet or Baritone 𝄞 . . . . Parès-Whistler

French Horn, E♭ Alto or Mellophone . . . . Parès-Whistler

Trombone or Baritone 𝄢 . . . . Parès-Whistler

E♭ Bass (Tuba - Sousaphone) . . . . Parès-Whistler

● BB♭ Bass (Tuba - Sousaphone) . . . . Parès-Whistler

Marimba, Xylophone or Vibes . . . . Parès-Whistler-Jolliff

For Individual Study and Like-Instrument Class Instruction
(Not Playable by Bands or by Mixed-Instruments)

RUBANK®

HAL•LEONARD®
CORPORATION
7777 W BLUEMOUND RD P O BOX 13819 MILWAUKEE, WI 53213

Key of C Major

Long Tones to Strengthen Lips

Scale of C

Also practice holding each tone for EIGHT counts.
When playing long tones, practice (1) $\diagup$ and (2) $\diagdown$.

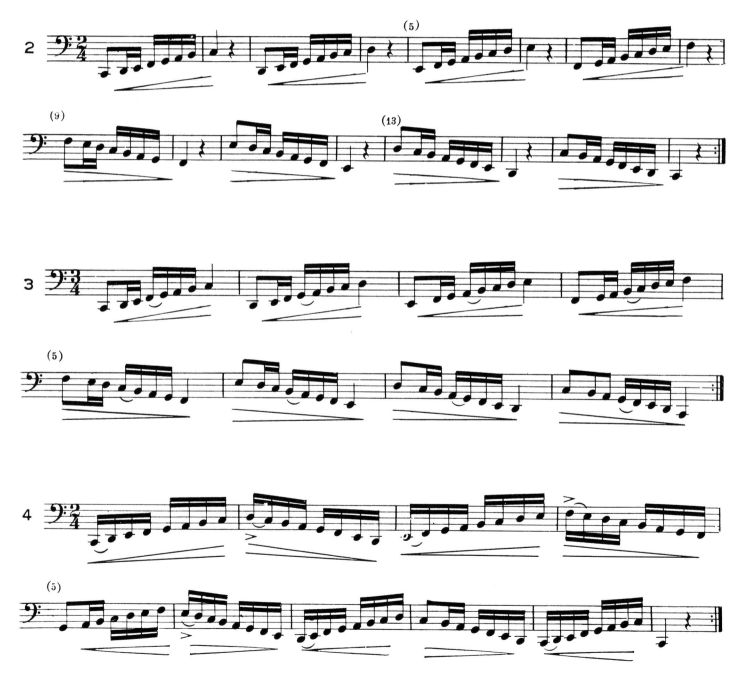

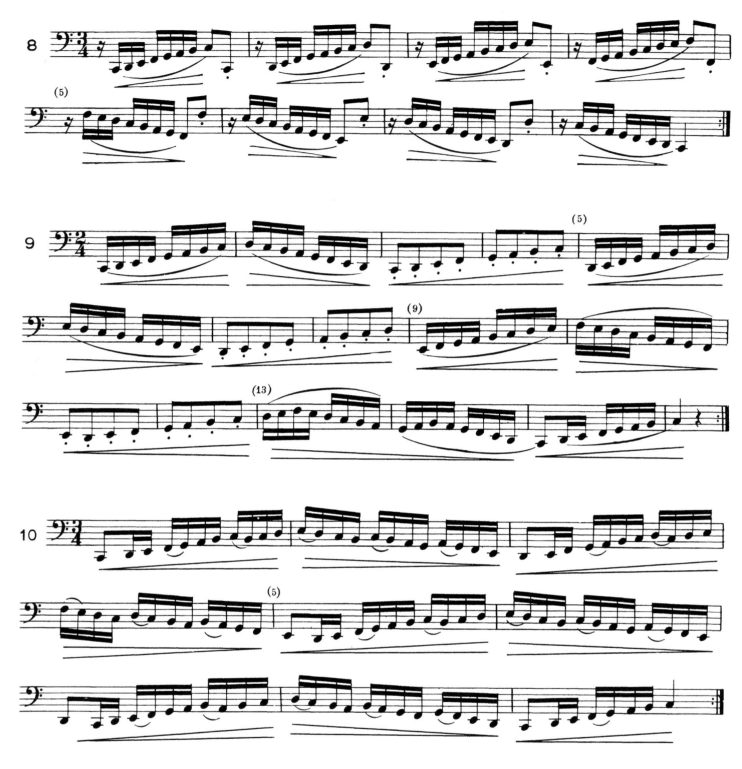

Embouchure Studies

Slur as many tones as possible. Also practice tonguing each tone.

Slur as many tones as possible. Also practice tonguing each tone.

Key of F Major

Long Tones to Strengthen Lips

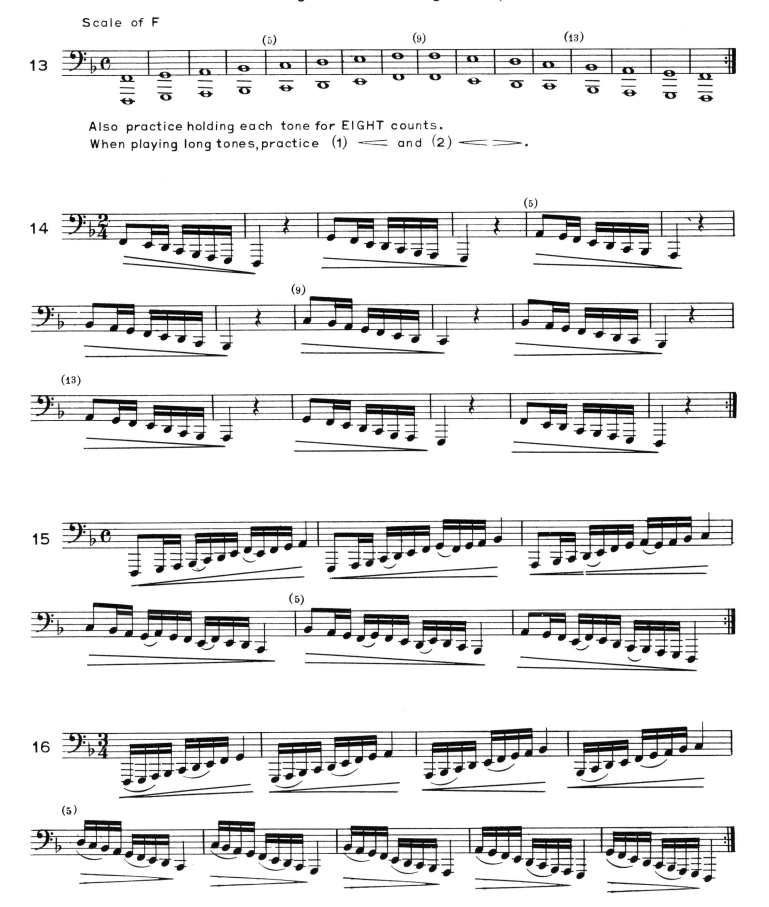

Scale of F

Also practice holding each tone for EIGHT counts.
When playing long tones, practice (1) ⤚ and (2) ⤚⤜.

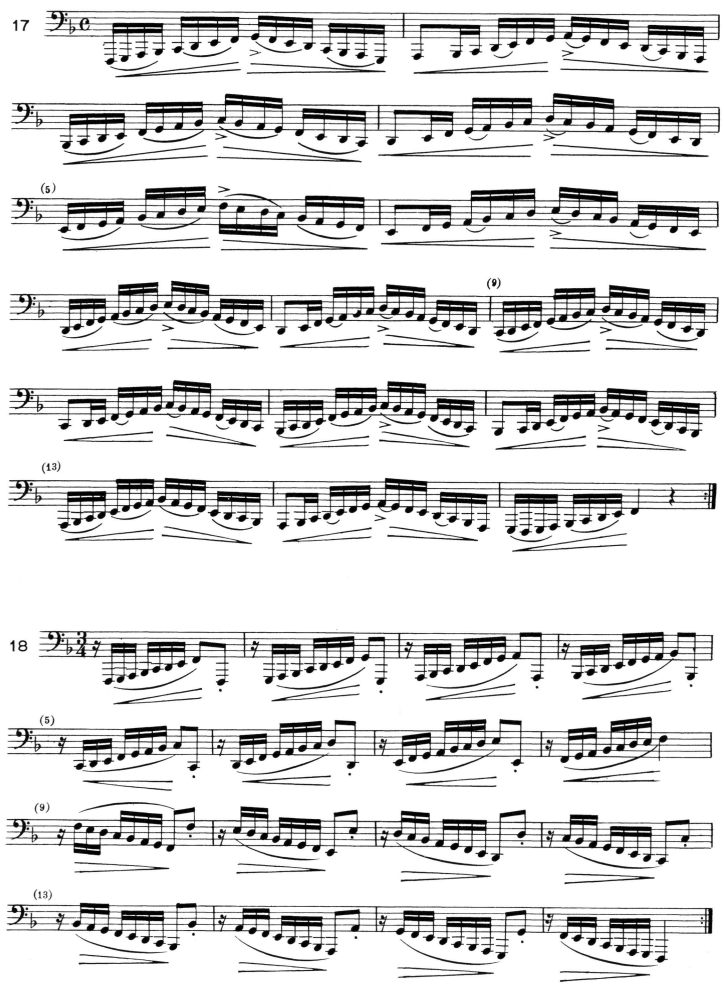

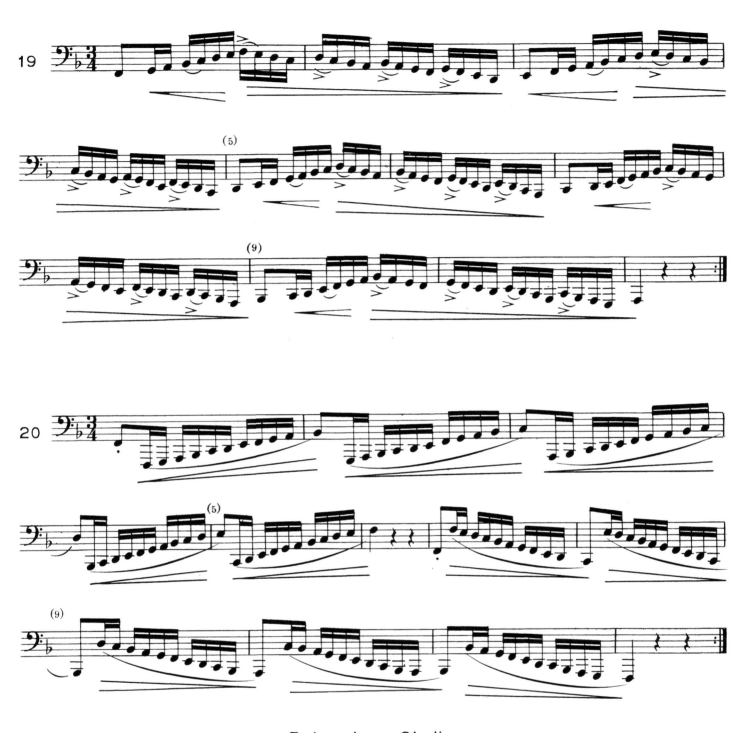

Embouchure Studies

Slur as many tones as possible. Also practice tonguing each tone.

Slur as many tones as possible. Also practice tonguing each tone.

Key of G Major

Long Tones to Strengthen Lips

Scale of G

Also practice holding each tone for EIGHT counts.
When playing long tones, practice (1) ⏥ and (2) ⏥ .

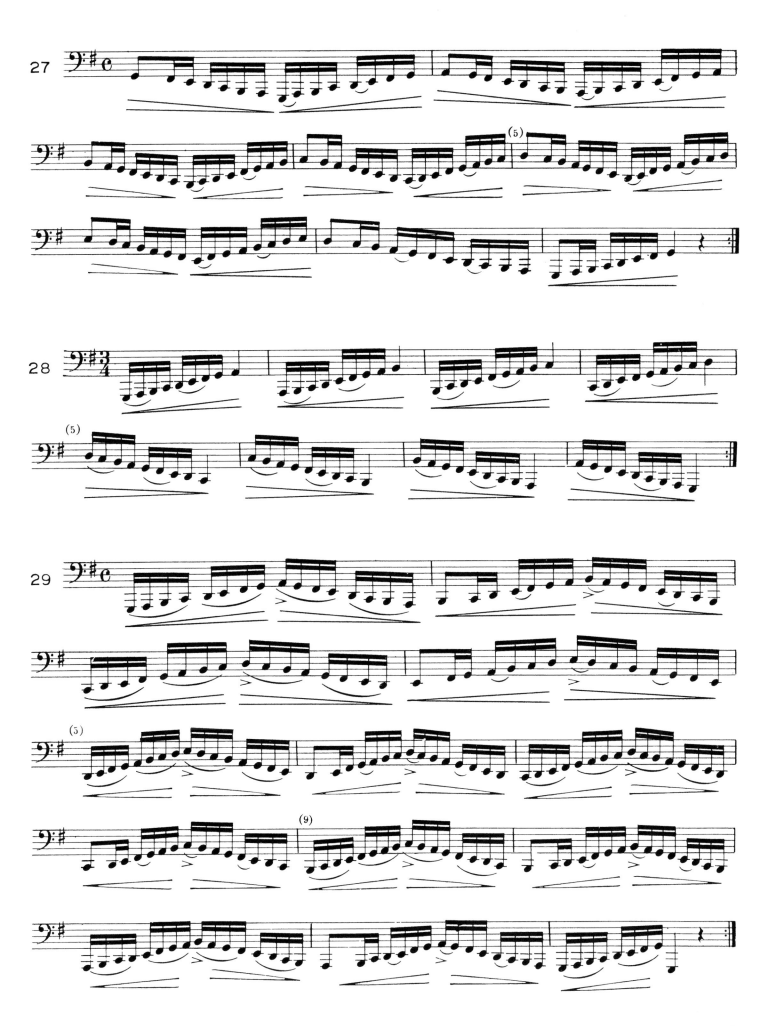

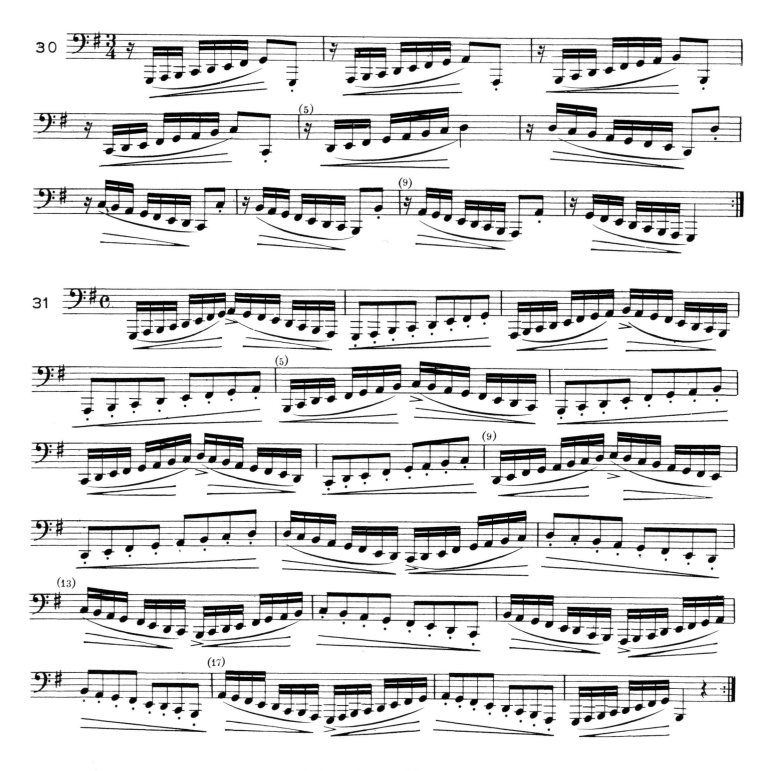

Embouchure Studies

Slur as many tones as possible. Also practice tonguing each tone.

Slur as many tones as possible. Also practice tonguing each tone.

Key of B♭ Major

Long Tones to Strengthen Lips

Scale of B♭

Also practice holding each tone for EIGHT counts.
When playing long tones, practice (1) ⟨ and (2) ⟨⟩ .

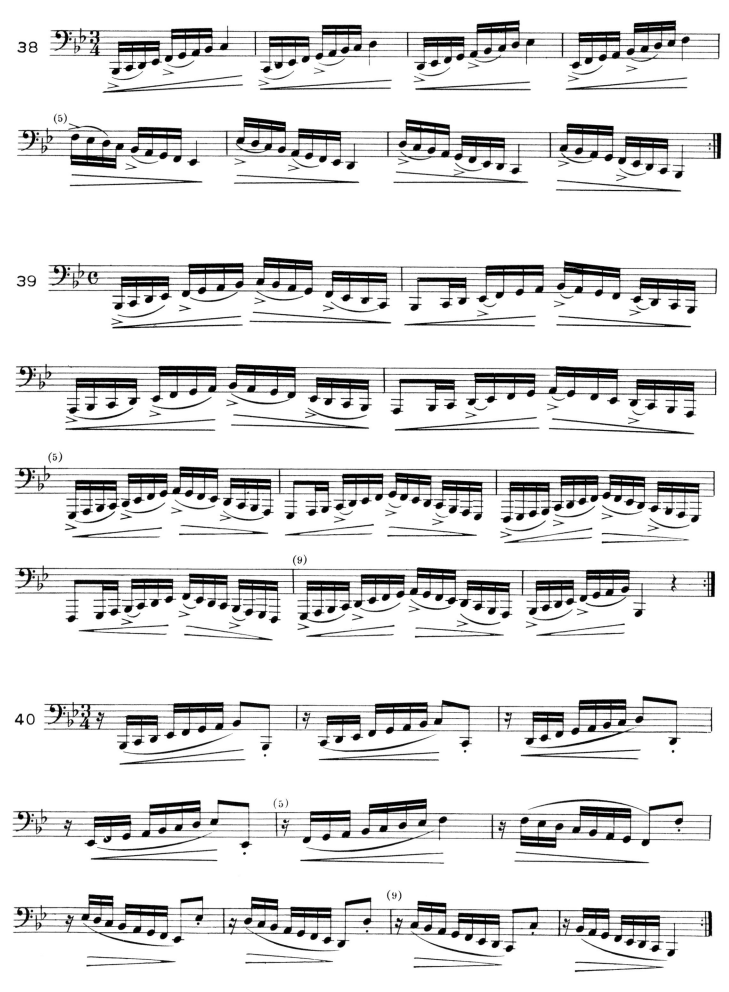

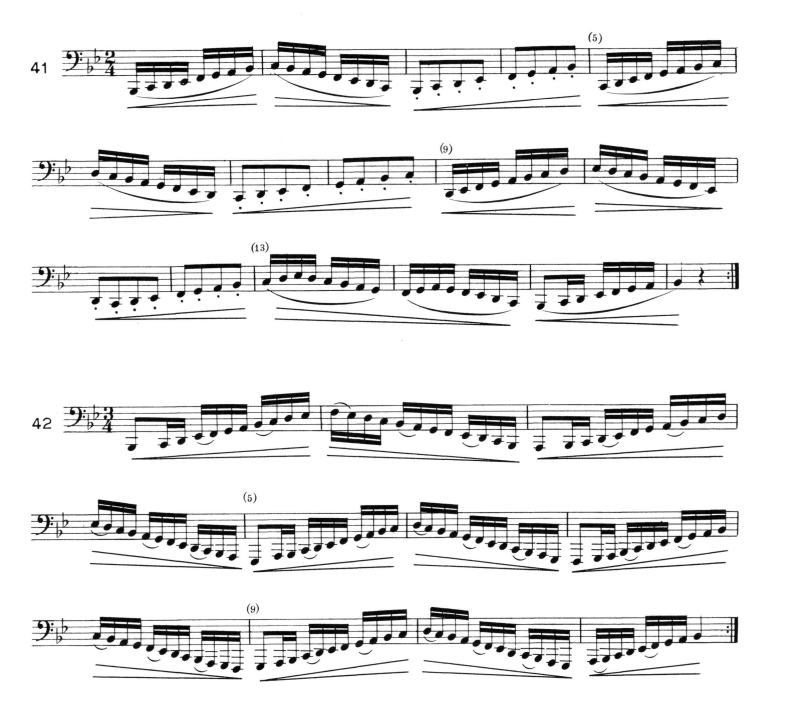

Embouchure Studies

Slur as many tones as possible. Also practice tonguing each tone.

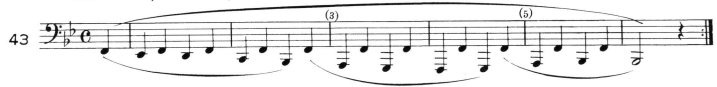

Slur as many tones as possible. Also practice tonguing each tone.

Key of D Major

Long Tones to Strengthen Lips

Scale of D

Also practice holding each tone for EIGHT counts.
When playing long tones, practice (1) ⟨ and (2) ⟨⟩.

Embouchure Studies

Slur as many tones as possible. Also practice tonguing each tone.

Slur as many tones as possible. Also practice tonguing each tone.

Key of E♭ Major

Long Tones to Strengthen Lips

Also practice holding each tone for EIGHT counts.
When playing long tones, practice (1) ◁ and (2) ◁▷.

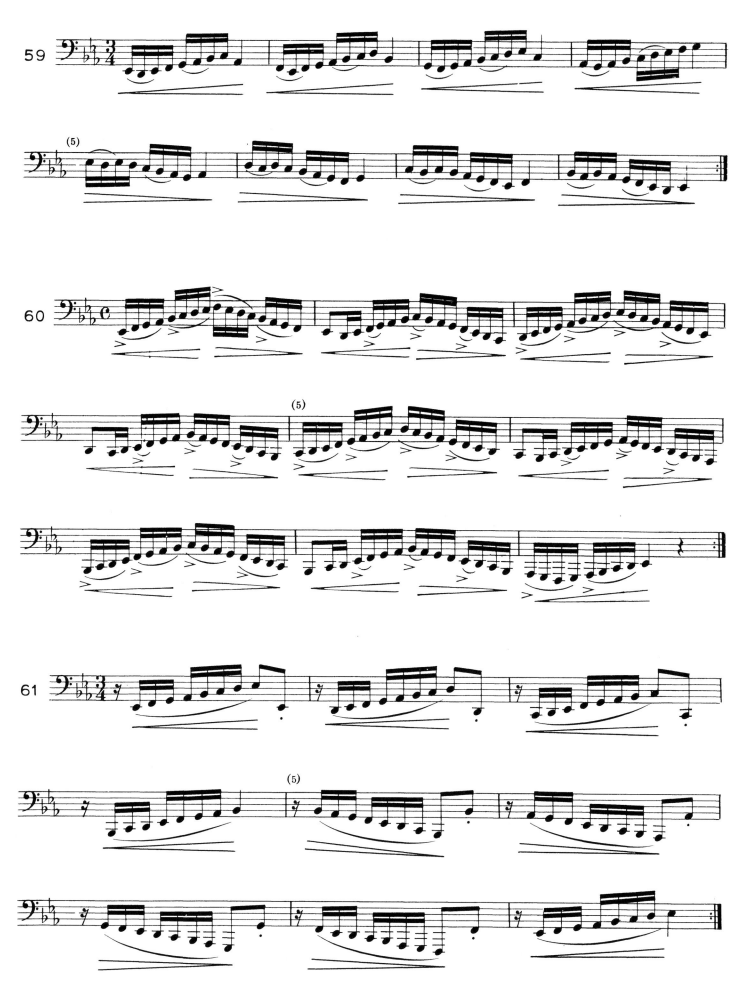

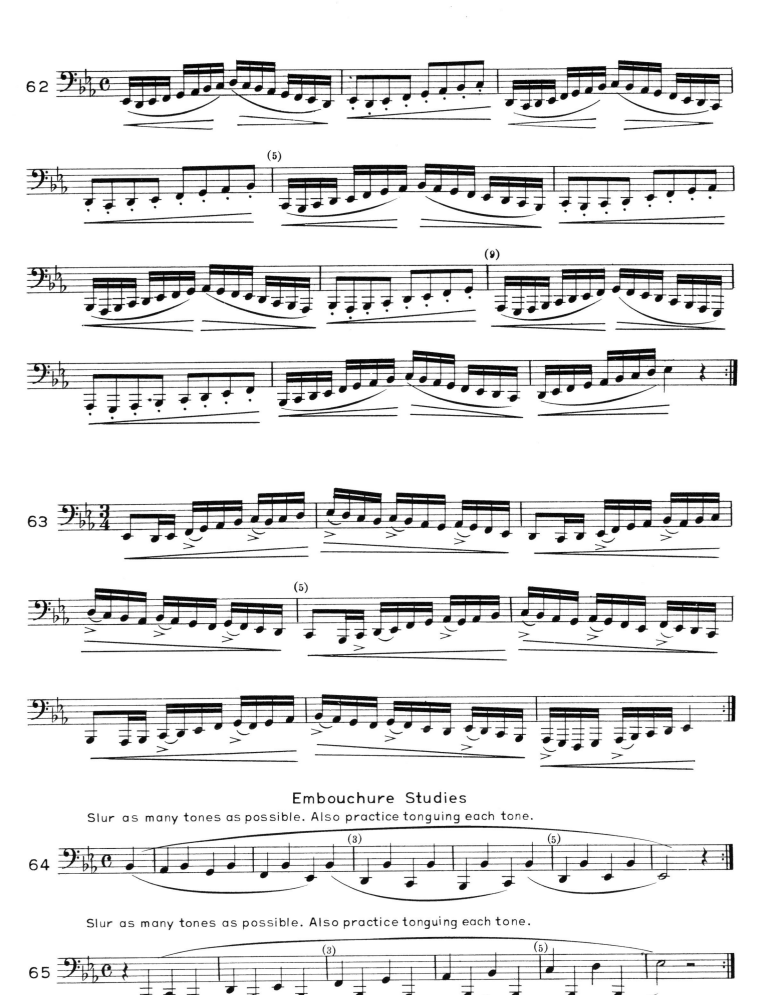

Embouchure Studies

Slur as many tones as possible. Also practice tonguing each tone.

Slur as many tones as possible. Also practice tonguing each tone.

Key of A Major

Long Tones to Strengthen Lips

Scale of A

Also practice holding each tone for EIGHT counts.
When playing long tones, practice (1) ⟨ and (2) ⟨⟩.

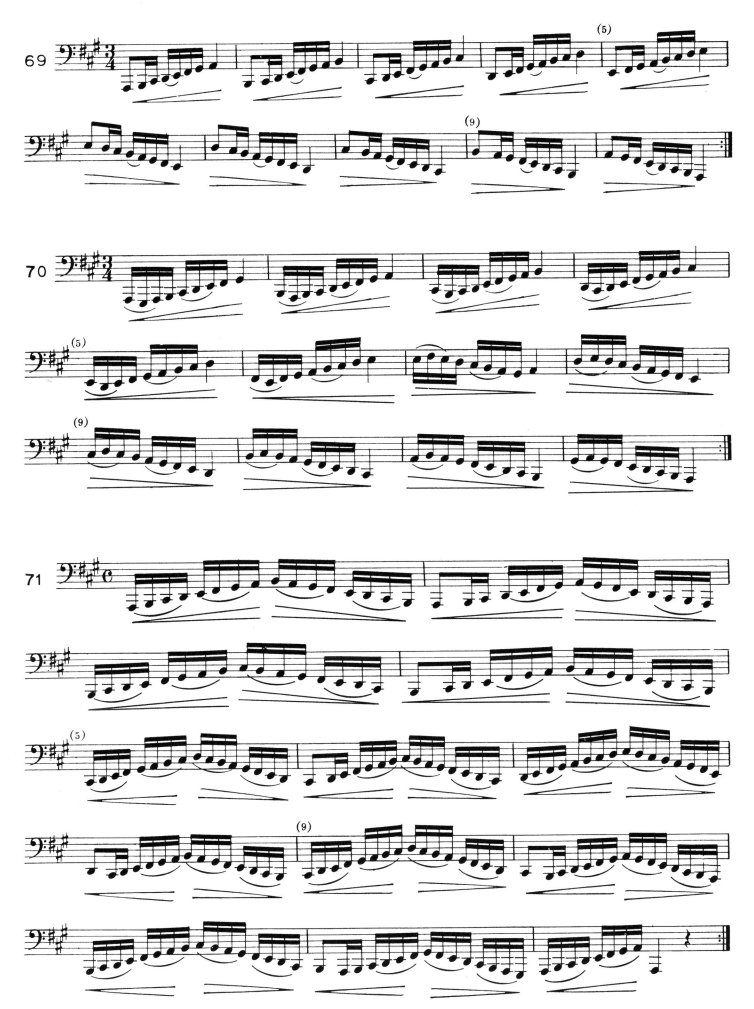

Embouchure Studies

Slur as many tones as possible. Also practice tonguing each tone.

Slur as many tones as possible. Also practice tonguing each tone.

Key of A♭ Major

Long Tones to Strengthen Lips

Scale of A♭

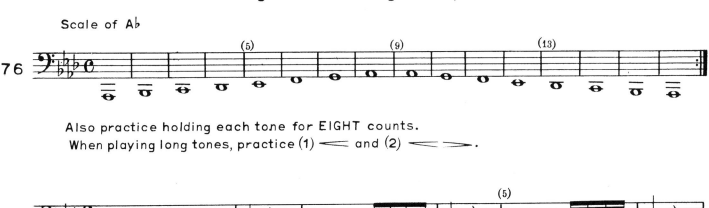

76

Also practice holding each tone for EIGHT counts.
When playing long tones, practice (1) ⟨ and (2) ⟨ ⟩.

77

78

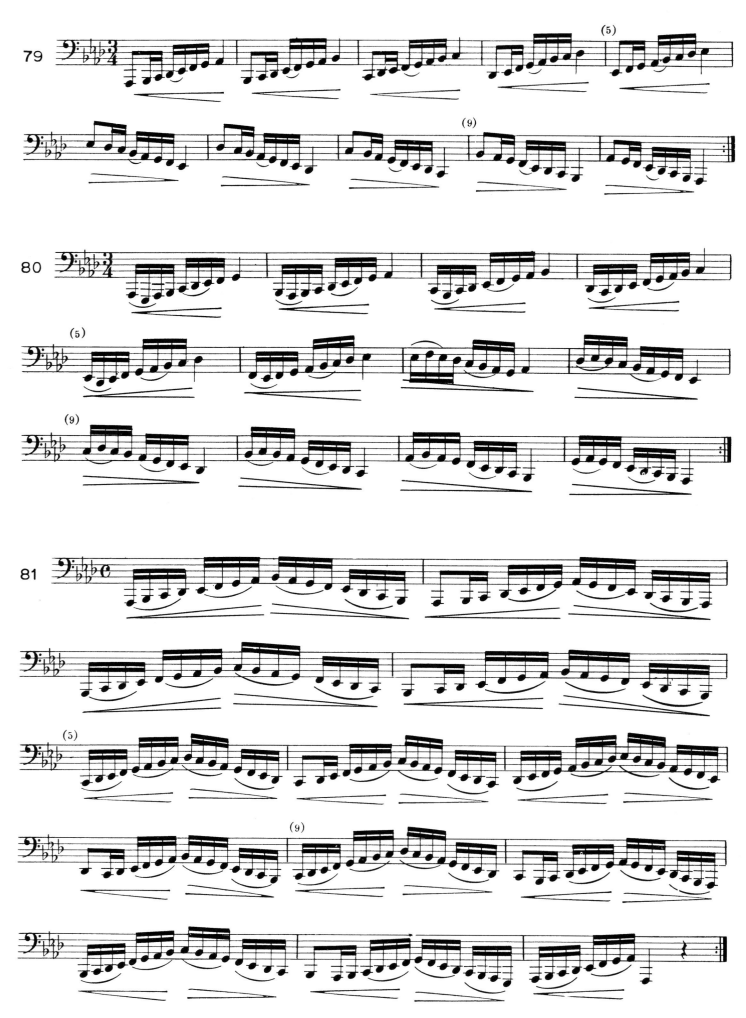

Embouchure Studies

Slur as many tones as possible. Also practice tonguing each tone

Slur as many tones as possible. Also practice tonguing each tone.

Key of D♭ Major

Long Tones to Strengthen Lips

Scale of D♭

Also practice holding each tone for EIGHT counts.
When playing long tones, practice (1) ⟨ and (2) ⟨⟩.

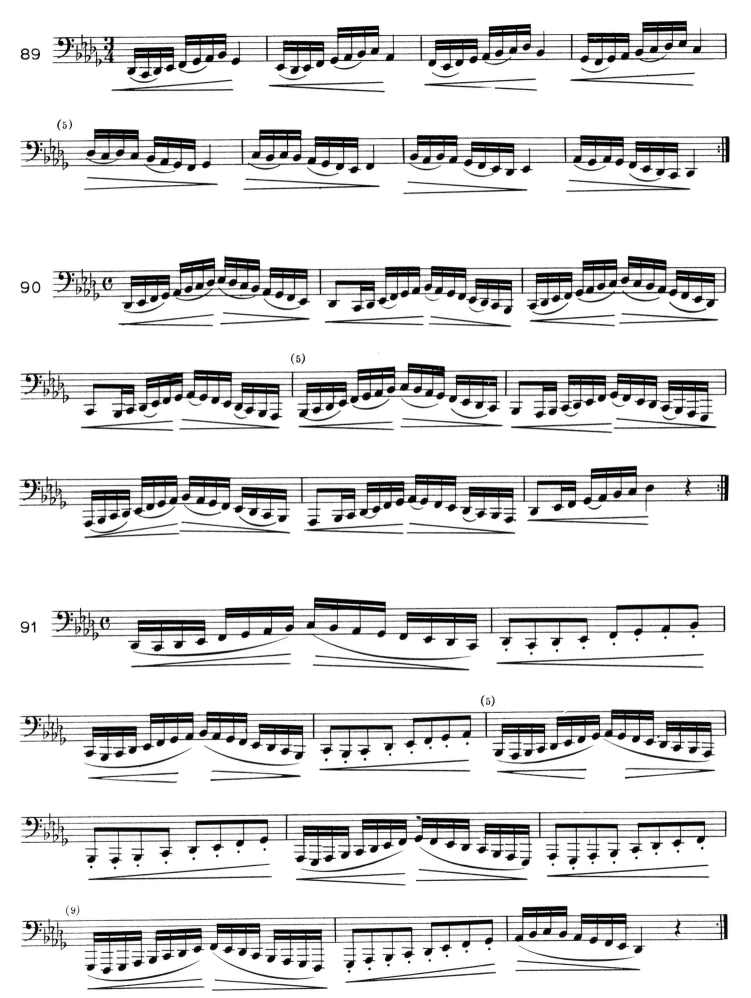

Embouchure Studies

Slur as many tones as possible. Also practice tonguing each tone.

Slur as many tones as possible. Also practice tonguing each tone.

Key of A Minor
(Relative to the Key of C Major)

Long Tones to Strengthen Lips

Scale of A Harmonic Minor

96

Scale of A Melodic Minor

97

Also practice holding each tone for EIGHT counts.
When playing long tones, practice (1) —◁ and (2) ◁—▷

98

99

Embouchure Studies

Slur as many tones as possible. Also practice tonguing each tone.

100

Slur as many tones as possible. Also practice tonguing each tone.

101

Key of D Minor
(Relative to the Key of F Major)

Long Tones to Strengthen Lips

Scale of D Harmonic Minor

Scale of D Melodic Minor

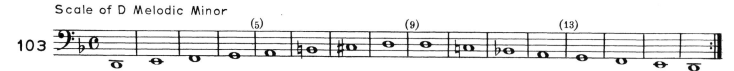

Also practice holding each tone for EIGHT counts.
When playing long tones, practice (1) ⟨ and (2) ⟨⟩

Embouchure Studies

Slur as many tones as possible. Also practice tonguing each tone.

Slur as many tones as possible. Also practice tonguing each tone.

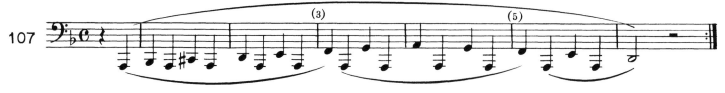

Key of E Minor
(Relative to the Key of G Major)

Long Tones to Strengthen Lips

Scale of E Harmonic Minor

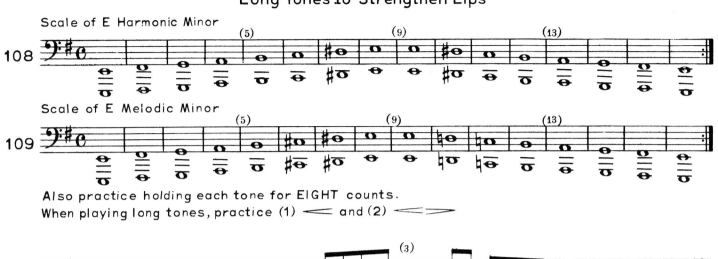

Scale of E Melodic Minor

Also practice holding each tone for EIGHT counts.
When playing long tones, practice (1) and (2)

Embouchure Studies

Slur as many tones as possible. Also practice tonguing each tone.

Slur as many tones as possible. Also practice tonguing each tone.

Key of G Minor
(Relative to the Key of B♭ Major)

Long Tones to Strengthen Lips

Scale of G Harmonic Minor

Scale of G Melodic Minor

Also practice holding each tone for EIGHT counts.
When playing long tones, practice (1) ⟨ and (2) ⟨⟩.

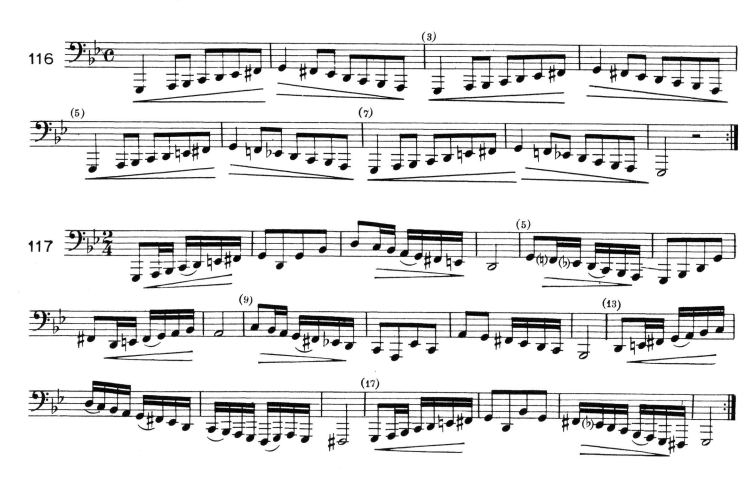

Embouchure Studies

Slur as many tones as possible. Also practice tonguing each tone.

Slur as many tones as possible. Also practice tonguing each tone.

Key of B Minor
(Relative to the Key of D Major)

Long Tones to Strengthen Lips

Scale of B Harmonic Minor

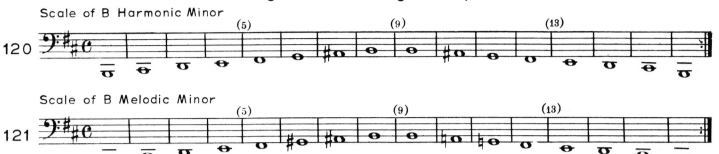

Scale of B Melodic Minor

Also practice holding each tone for EIGHT counts.
When playing long tones, practice (1) and (2).

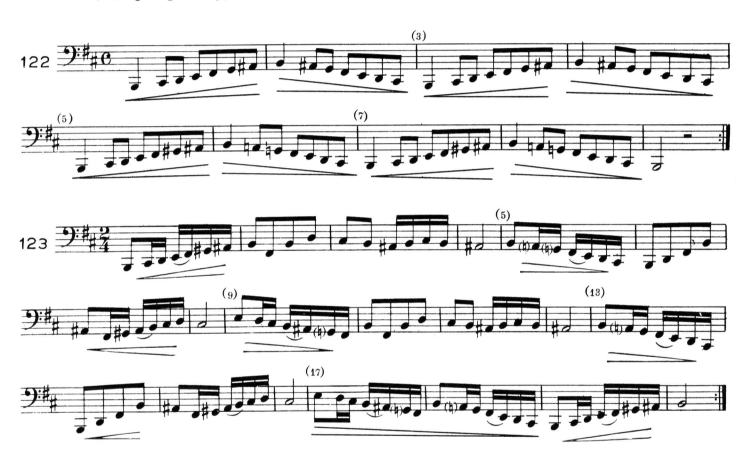

Embouchure Studies

Slur as many tones as possible. Also practice tonguing each tone.

Slur as many tones as possible. Also practice tonguing each tone.

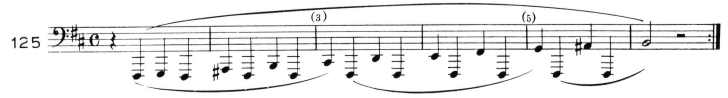

Key of C Minor
(Relative to the Key of E♭ Major)

Long Tones to Strengthen Lips

Scale of C Harmonic Minor

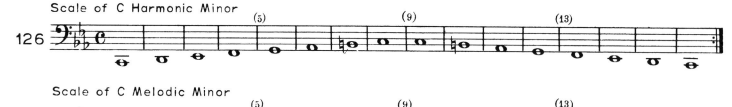

126

Scale of C Melodic Minor

127

Also practice holding each tone for EIGHT counts.
When playing long tones, practice (1) ⟨ and (2) ⟨ ⟩

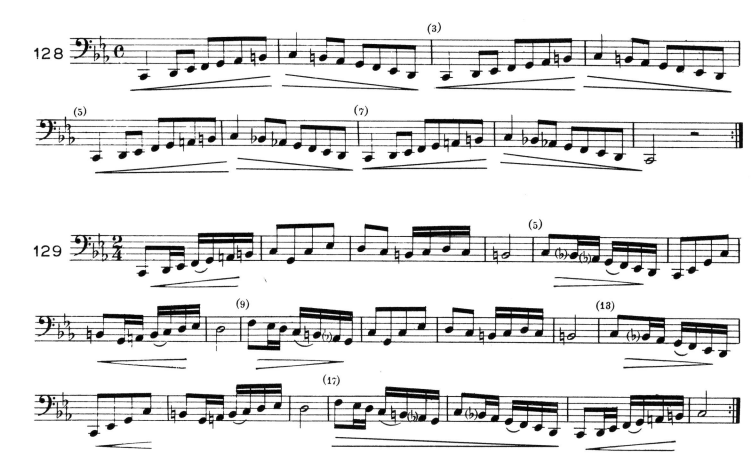

128

129

Embouchure Studies

Slur as many tones as possible. Also practice tonguing each tone.

130

Slur as many tones as possible. Also practice tonguing each tone.

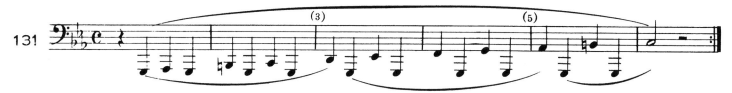

131

Key of F# Minor
(Relative to the Key of A Major)

Long Tones to Strengthen Lips

Scale of F# Harmonic Minor

132

Scale of F# Melodic Minor

133

Also practice holding each tone for EIGHT counts.
When playing long tones, practice (1) and (2).

134

135

Embouchure Studies

Slur as many tones as possible. Also practice tonguing each tone.

136

Slur as many tones as possible. Also practice tonguing each tone.

137

Key of F Minor
(Relative to the Key of A♭ Major)

Long Tones to Strengthen Lips

Scale of F Harmonic Minor

Scale of F Melodic Minor

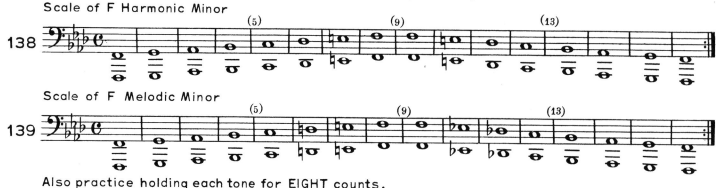

Also practice holding each tone for EIGHT counts.
When playing long tones, practice (1) < and (2) < >.

Embouchure Studies

Slur as many tones as possible. Also practice tonguing each tone.

Slur as many tones as possible. Also practice tonguing each tone.

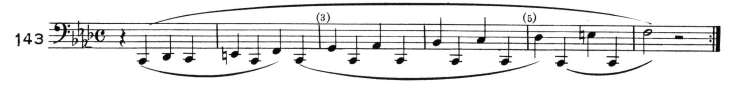

Key of B♭ Minor
(Relative to the Key of D♭ Major)

Long Tones to Strengthen Lips

Scale of B♭ Harmonic Minor

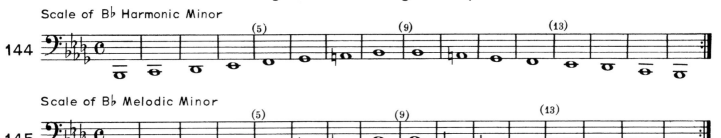

144

Scale of B♭ Melodic Minor

145

Also practice holding each tone for EIGHT counts.
When playing long tones, practice (1) ⟨ and (2) ⟨⟩.

146

147

Embouchure Studies

Slur as many tones as possible. Also practice tonguing each tone.

148

Slur as many tones as possible. Also practice tonguing each tone.

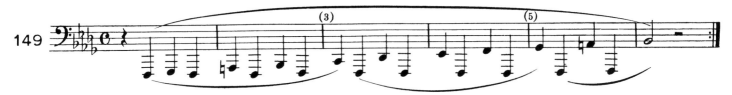

149

Major Scales

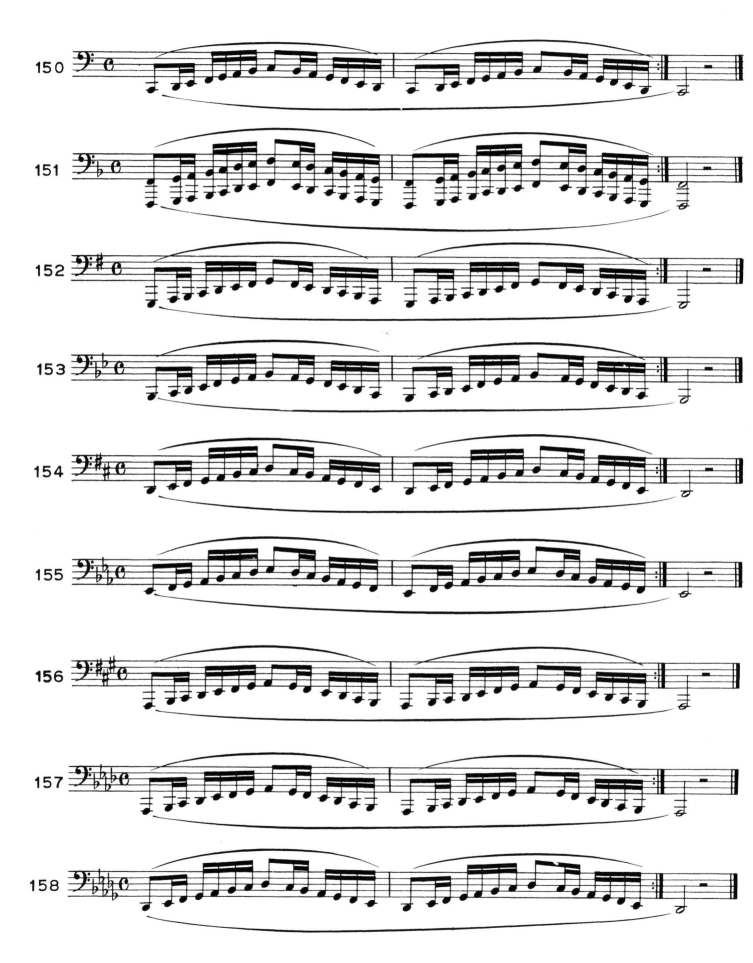

Harmonic Minor Scales

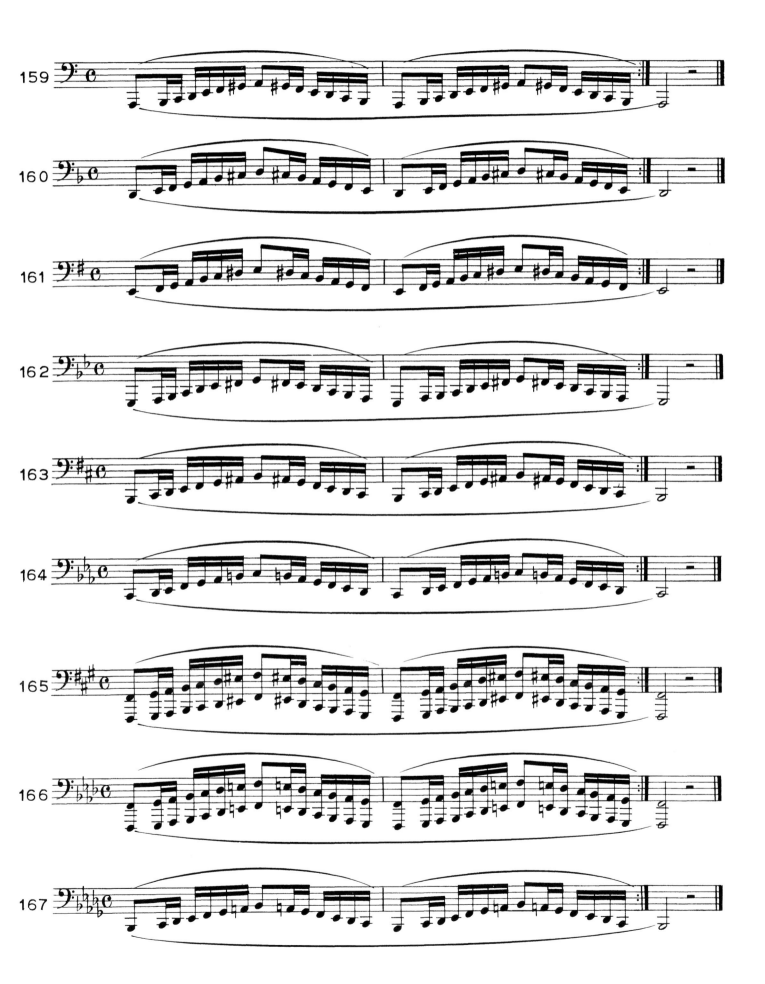

Melodic Minor Scales

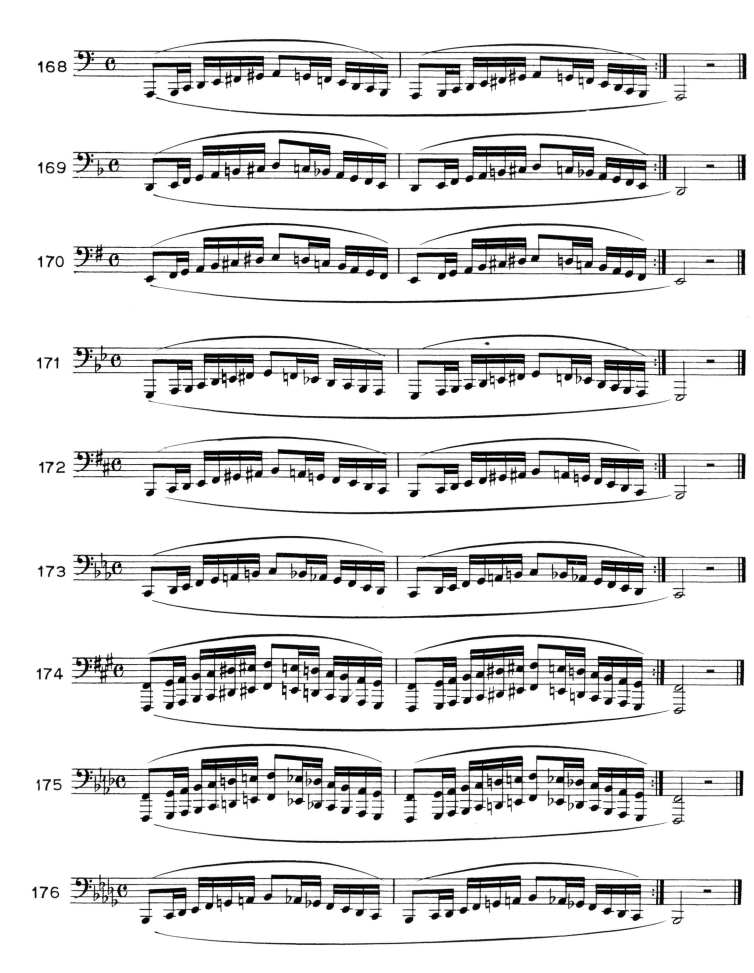

Arpeggios

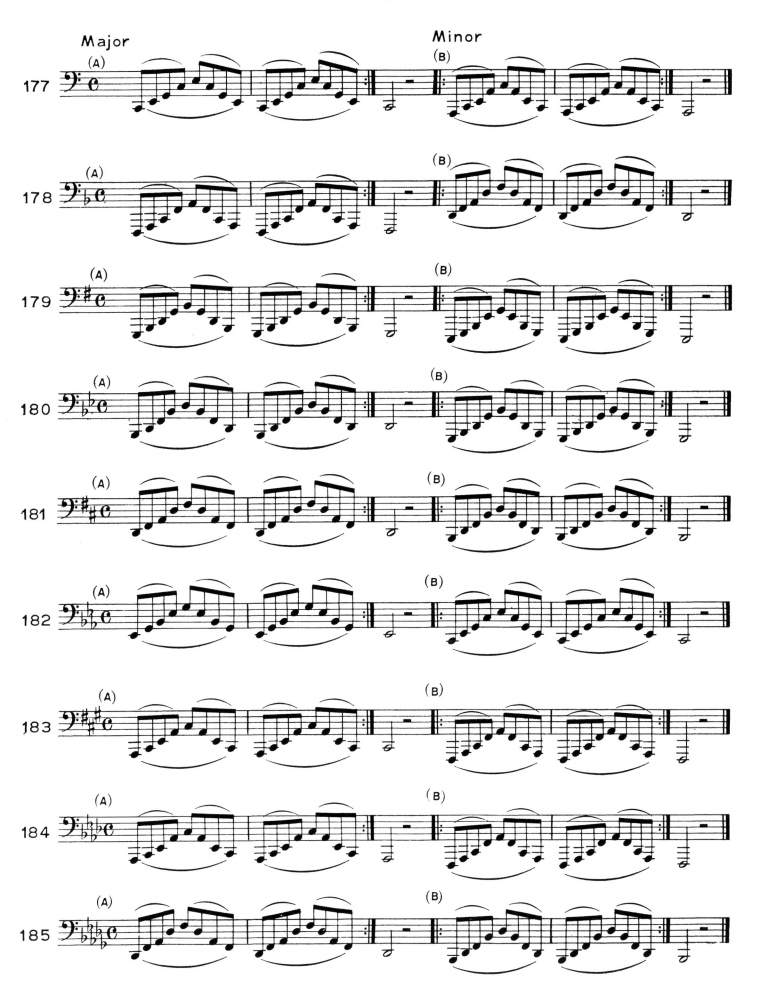

Chromatic Studies

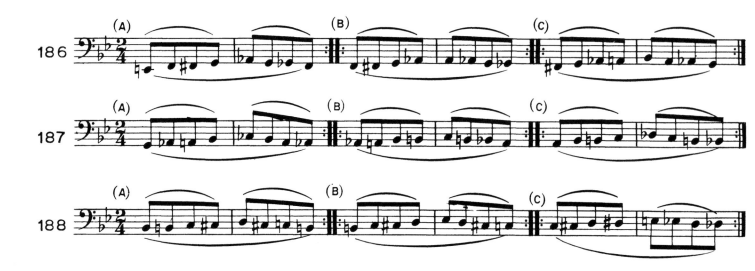

Chromatic Studies in Sixteenth Notes

Chromatic Studies in Triplets

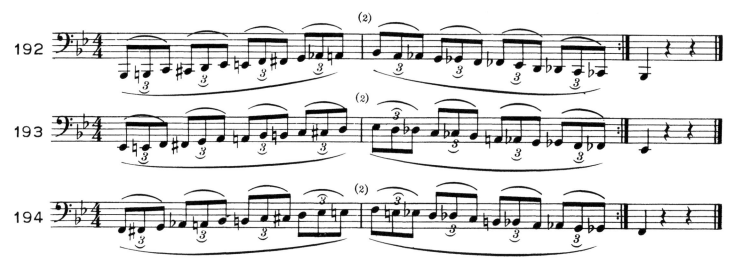

Chromatic Scales

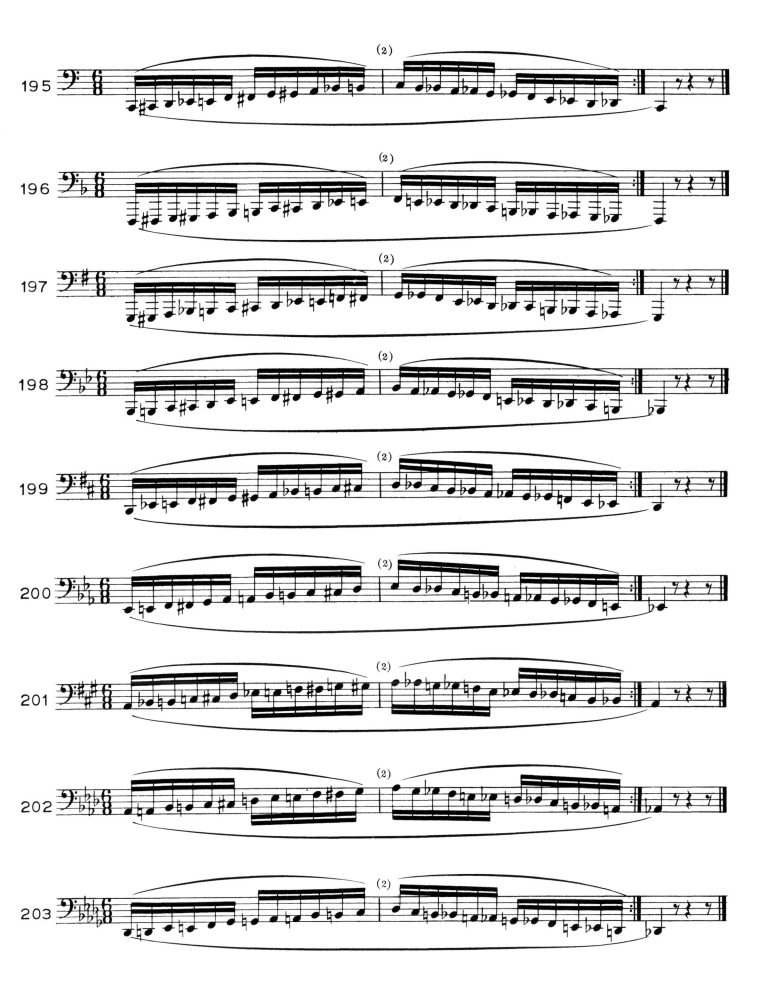

Basic Exercises to Develop Tones

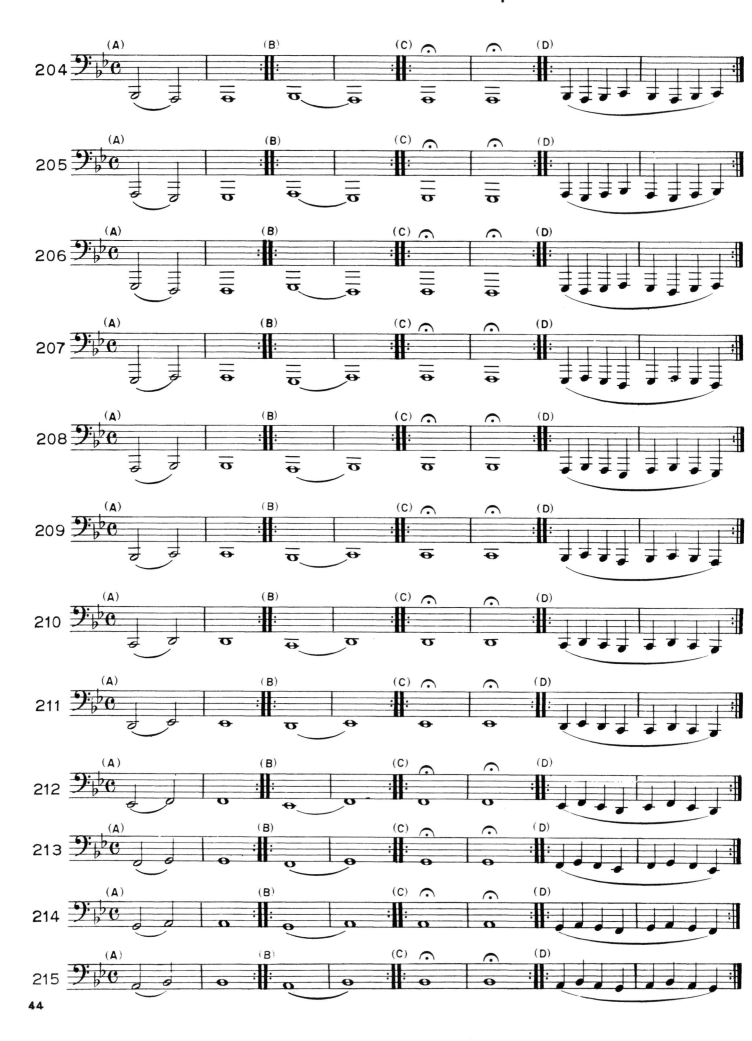

Basic Exercises to Strengthen Tones

(a) Also practice very slowly, holding each tone for (1) FOUR counts, and (2) EIGHT counts.

When playing long tones, practice (1) ⟨ and (2) ⟨⟩.

(b) Also practice very legato, (1) slurring each two tones, and (2) slurring each four tones.

Studies in Mechanism

Interval Exercises

Technic Builder No.1

Technic Builder No.2